D1220187

Scotland

TIGER BOOKS INTERNATIONAL

Text by
Isabella Brega

Graphic design
Anna Galliani

Map
Giancarlo Gellona

Contents

1 *The roof of Glamis Castle, former seat of the earls of Strathmore and Kinghorne and since 1372 a royal residence, offers a fine vantage point from which to admire the green hills all around.*

2-3 *A crofter's house in the vicinity of Leckfurin: the idyllic scenes offered by the Scottish countryside (totally detached from the stress and strain of city life) have always held enormous appeal for foreigners. Hollywood's movie-makers have certainly not been immune to the charms of this bucolic paradise, choosing it as the setting for films like the musical* Brigadoon, *produced by Vincent Minnelli in 1954.*

4-5 *Eilean Donan Castle too has become practically a shrine for movie buffs, after appearing in several scenes of the film* Highlander, *starring Christopher Lambert and Sean Connery. Said to be the most photographed castle in Scotland, it stands picturesquely on a tiny island. Seat of the Mackenzie Clan , it was built in 1230 on the ruins of previous fortifications; destroyed in the 1700s, it was restored in the early years of this century. It houses a small museum on the Jacobite period.*

6-7 *The lighthouse at Neist Point is a prominent landmark on the Hebridean island of Skye. This island was the scene of one of the best known and most romantic episodes in Scottish history: after his defeat in the bloody battle of Culloden in 1746, Charles Edward Stuart (the 'Bonnie Prince Charlie' of song and legend), pretender to the British crown, was sheltered here by Flora MacDonald, who thus enabled him to escape to exile in Italy.*

8 *Kilt Rock, a high cliff on the island of Skye, got its name from its unusual structure: vertically and horizontally stratified basalt creates a pattern that looks distinctly like a typical Scottish tartan.*

9 *The unicorn on the Mercat Cross (where proclamations were once made) is one of the symbols of Edinburgh, Scotland's capital.*

12-13 *This isolated farmstead is situated in the Grampians region, among glens where Scots pine trees - now increasingly rare - are a prevalent feature of the landscape. In this part of Scotland plentiful game (red deer, roe deer, grouse and pheasant) attracts sportsmen from all over the world.*

14-15 *Anstruther is a picturesque fishing port in the Fife region which extends into the North Sea between the Firth of Forth and the River Tay.*

16-17 *Built between 1500 and 1505, with a tall, lantern-topped belltower, the chapel is the most distinctive feature of King's College (1495), the oldest part of Aberdeen university. In terms of population, Aberdeen is Scotland's third largest city.*

This edition published in 1996 by TIGER BOOKS INTERNATIONAL PLC , 26a York Street Twickenham TW1 3LJ, England.

First published by Edizioni White Star. Title of the original edition: Scozia, l'orgogliosa fierezza di un popolo millenario.
© World copyright 1996 by Edizioni White Star, Via Candido Sassone 22/24, 13100 Vercelli, Italy.

This edition reproduced by permission of White Star Edizioni. All rights reserved. No part of this publication may be reproduced, stored in a retrieval system, or transmitted in any form by any means, electronic, mechanical, photocopying or otherwise, without first obtaining written permission of the copyright owner.

ISBN 1-85501-816-0

Printed in Singapore by Tien Wah Press. Color separations by Graphic Service, Milano, Italy.

Orkney
Islands

The Minch

Thurso

Loch Shin.

Hebrides

▲
Beinn Dearg

Moray Firth

Skye

HIGHLAND

Spey

Carn Eige
▲

Loch Ness

Ben Macdhui
▲

ABERDEEN ●

Beinn Fhada
▲

Monadhliath
Mountains

Dee

Loch Arkaig

Sgurrna Ciohe

Loch Laggan

Grampians

Loch Ericht

ATLANTIC OCEAN

Loch Shiel

Ben Alder
▲

Lochnagar
▲

Ben Nevis
▲

Loch Rannoch

Glas Maol
▲

Ben Lawers

Loch Tay

DUNDEE ●

Mull

Ben More
▲

Loch Earn

Loch Katrine

Loch Awe

Loch Leven

Jura

A R G Y L L

Loch Lomond

KIRKCALDY ●

Firth of Forth

Greenock

EDINBURGH

Islay

Paisley

Coatbridge

GLASGOW ●

Motherwell

Kintyre

Arran

Firth of Clyde

Campbeltown

SOUTHERN
UPLANDS

IRELAND

NORTHERN
IRELAND

North Channel

DUMFRIES

GALLOWAY

ENGLAND

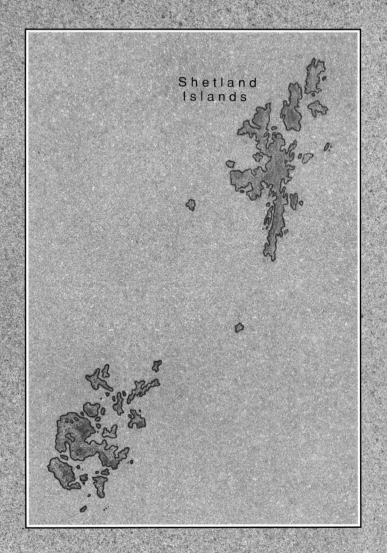

Shetland
Islands

NORTH SEA

Introduction

It was not until well into the 19th century - and thanks to an Englishwoman - that people south of the border started to regard Scotland as a significant place on the map. The woman in question was Queen Victoria, no less... occupant of the throne once held by the ruthless Elizabeth I who, in 1587, after keeping in captivity for twenty years her 'inconvenient' Catholic Scottish cousin, Mary Stuart - the deposed Mary Queen of Scots - had her beheaded for fear she might lay claim to the English crown. There had always been bad blood between the two countries. A tough, proud race, the Scots had never really been subdued by the far more sophisticated English who, in 1707, made this land the northernmost part of Great Britain.

For Victoria it was love at first sight. Advised that the dry air of the Scottish mountains would do wonders for her rheumatism, she made her first visit to this neglected outpost of her reign in 1842, and instantly fell for its charms. Hence her wish for her own "corner of paradise" in the northerly Highlands, a wild mountainous region with few inhabitants besides Cheviot sheep. A comfortable, intimate haven, far removed from the pomp - and chilly interiors - of Buckingham Palace, where bureaucracy reigned: the palace department which procured fuel had little or nothing to do with staff responsible for lighting fires. The often disastrous outcome was that here, as at Windsor Castle, the queen was forced to walk miles along galleries and corridors solely to keep herself warm.

Her choice fell upon Balmoral, in the Grampian Mountains: a small castle surrounded by a vast estate, built in Scottish Baronial style to meet the needs of her fast growing family (she and Albert, the Prince Consort, already had seven children). Work on extending the castle was completed in 1856 and for six years the royal family made it their autumn residence, a centre for excursions incognito, deer hunting and salmon fishing. After personal involvement in the design of the building itself, Prince Albert let his creative

impulse loose on the interior decor: maplewood furniture with silver locks and hinges, horrific candelabra made from stag horns on porcelain supports decorated with figures of Highlanders, and ubiquitous tartan (to the Prince's own designs) for curtains, wall coverings and carpets, even in the Queen's bedroom. The seeds had been sown. Flattered by so much regal attention, Scots at large began to adopt as national symbols what had previously been considered to belong strictly to the 'barbarous' clans of the Highlands: kilts, tartan (with everyone desperate to get their own personal pattern), bagpipes, tam-o'-shanters, eagle feathers and the inevitable sprigs of dried heather.

South of the border, Her Majesty's loyal subjects were soon following in her footsteps. Already familiar with works of art and literature that sang Scotland's praises - the false Ossianic sagas of Macpherson, the romantic novels of Scott, poems by the 'Lake District poets', Wordsworth and Coleridge, paintings by Nasmyth - they now noticed another gem in the Empire's crown. They discovered a magical land suspended between sky and water, in sharp contrast to the oppressive heat of Indian summers and the fragrant spices and teas of the East India Company. Improved communications lending a hand, London's aristocrats dashed north to contend for ownership of the most attractive castles and estates. A new fashion had been launched, and it very quickly acquired further essential trappings: intensely green golf courses (the oldest and finest in the world), colourful tartans with their neat checks, kilts and accompanying folklore, droning notes of bagpipes, fragrant peat, tasty butter shortbread and warming whisky. Now familiar to one and all, this hotchpotch image of Scotland smacks more of kitsch than of class but even the Scots themselves have, in some respects, come to identify with it.

If Victoria did more than her fair share to heighten Scotland's popularity, Nature did the rest. Thanks to the fascination of its hostile physical features, Scotland succeeded in passing the dividing line beyond which a barren landscape becomes picturesque, a rugged earthly paradise where nature still exists in the raw. Perhaps the Scots themselves had been the first to realize this: they were undoubtedly skilful in turning the

18 *The valley of Corgarff Castle* (top) *and a river flowing toward Kentallen Bay* (centre photo) *- has charmed poets and artists, men of letters and aristocrats, kings and queens. And it was in fact the English queen Victoria who started a fashion that secured a triumphant new image for 19th-century Scotland. London's aristocrats quickly succumbed to the subtle spell worked by mist-shrouded castles, wild, barren countryside, mountains and glens mirrored in still lochs: assisted by improved communications with this neglected corner of the British Isles, they outdid one another in their frenetic desire to buy up estates and stately homes, dress up in kilts and tartans and dedicate their leisure to shooting and fishing.*

19 *Scotland's magic is fully revealed when the works of man are dwarfed by the splendour of nature in the wild. Its scenic beauty is often stunning: rivers and lochs, windswept villages, waterfalls (above, on the River Shiel) or isolated homesteads (like the croft pictured in the photo below, not far from Inverbain).*

20-21 *The celebrated Military Tatoo is held on the esplanade of Edinburgh Castle during the annual international Edinburgh Festival. During the three weeks of the festival, in August, the Scottish capital is invaded by performers in official and 'Fringe' events: actors, musicians, singers, puppeteers, pipers (playing bagpipes, of course), dancers, jugglers, clowns and every other possible kind of entertainer.*

fashion set by their majestic guest to their advantage. Much of the groundwork for the new romantic myth of the Highlands had already been laid by their compatriot, novelist Sir Walter Scott who, in 1822, convinced King George IV to cover his rotund form (120 kilos...) with Royal Stewart tartan. The first English sovereign to visit Edinburgh since Charles II, he appeared at the parade in his honour dressed in a kilt which came well below his knees, worn (just in case...) over flesh-coloured tights. But even he could not outshine the equally well-upholstered Lord Mayor of London, who took the precaution of wearing a kilt that practically reached his ankles. The Hollywood-style show ably mounted by Scott had all the essential ingredients: bagpipes, Gaelic, tartan, clans - and de rigueur kilts. The English had banned all these trappings of Scottish nationalism after the rebellion of 1745 and yet less than a century later, they were "borrowing" them as eye-catching emblems of their own national culture.

The real character of Scotland is revealed in its magnificent scenery and age-old traditions: as green as its golf courses, cold and crystal-clear like its lakes and rivers, volatile as its mists, as golden as its whisky, austere like its tartans, as solitary as the disquieting notes of its bagpipes, strong and rugged like its unconquered castles, fleeting like its ghosts. The proverbial stinginess of its people, perhaps justifiably reluctant to part with their precious resources, is another ingredient of the stereotypical Scot: together with hard work and original ideas, it has perhaps contributed to the fame and fortune of many who left their homeland to settle in the four corners of the globe (two "American" success stories - Campbell canned soup and MacDonald fast-food - say it all...). Scotland undoubtedly lives up to its legends, embedded deep in an amalgam of historic fact and myth. Tales from its past are often black and bloody, their protagonists marked by tragedies beyond our wildest imagination. How could we forget the cruel destiny of Mary Stuart, a wilful, rebellious, passionate yet pious woman? Or the handsome Bonnie Prince Charlie who, exiled after his desperate unsuccessful attempt to regain the throne, drowned his sorrows in drink? Or the brooding Macbeth, assassin of King Duncan, tormented by witches, bubbling cauldrons, foreboding signs and ubiquitous spots of blood? Men and women who followed the dictates of a troubled, untamed spirit and were unable to evade their tragic fate... the stuff of literary Romanticism turned into flesh and blood. Figures of the past whose stories of strife, passion and suffering unfold in a scenario blurred by mist, swept by gales, veiled by rain or illuminated by milky-white light beneath a leaden sky.

Scotland is a land shaped by heather and tears, peat and blood, barley and pride; a place where men's eyes speak of stormy seas while their womenfolk tell of anguished, lonely months spent waiting; where melancholy hangs heavy in the air as troubled souls wander aimlessly across barren moors and along paths thick with rain-sodden leaves, spied upon by fairies and gnomes, witches and monsters. It is a harsh land in which the timelessness of the moorlands contrasts with flowing waters and shifting mists, in which reality is coloured by enchantment, history becomes legend, pragmatism gives way to emotion. Few manage to resist the subtle spell cast by fields of waving golden grain, velvety green pastures, rocky hills, silent villages, islands by the tens and hundreds, medieval towns, neolithic dolmens, austere abbeys. And the magnificent world of its thousands of lochs and waters, crystalline or turbid, luminous or dark, still or threatening: castles or solitary ruins on their banks are mirrored in many of their surfaces; others glimmer in the sunlight or conceal dark secrets.

Water holds the key to Scotland and its majestic scenery: the waters of its lochs, its hundreds of rivers and its eight hundred islands; the water which soaks through its soil and makes its fields and pastures fertile; the rushing water challenged by salmon as they battle their way upstream to give life to a new generation. Scotland also offers us the quintessential "water of life", acquavitae, the 'uisge beatha' first distilled in Scotland and Ireland by Celtic monks: whisky, lifelong companion of Scots the world over. It is traditionally drunk with a glass of water (although a saying says "there are two things Scots like straight, and one is malt whisky") when eating haggis (the national dish, made from sheep's heart and liver mixed with spices, oatmeal and onion and stuffed into the lining of a sheep's stomach, traditionally eaten on Burns Night, January 25, to celebrate the birthday of 18th-century Scottish poet Robert Burns). A teaspoonful welcomes

babies into the world; several rounds see the deceased on their way into the next; and on New Year's Eve whisky, symbolizing life - together with salt for prosperity and coal for warmth - accompany the dark-haired man who, by tradition, must be first over the threshold of every house.

When vine pest left the upper échelons of English society without French cognac and wine, Victoria introduced them to the delights of Scotch whisky and a new fashion was started. The Queen's penchant for whisky was perhaps not unrelated to another royal passion by the name of John Brown, an unsophisticated Highland gamekeeper who, after the death of her beloved Prince Albert, reportedly won a place in her heart. It became tradition for every member of game shooting parties organized at Balmoral to be given a bottle of Scotch. And, by order of the Queen herself, a bottle was kept under the coachman's seat on all royal carriages: the 'sovereign remedy', constantly at hand. The queen liked to drink her whisky neat, in tea or with spring water (though she was also known to add a drop even to a splendid Bordeaux). In more than one instance she was herself described on bottle labels as 'The Queen of Scotch Whiskies'. When, in 1923, the Japanese first moved into the whisky distilling business (and, apart from Irish and American distillers, they alone have succeeded in creating a fine-quality light whisky, suited to Japanese palates), their marketing hype ran to such phrases as "the famous Scotch of Queen George VIII" and "King Victoria's pocket" and they even passed themselves off as "Purveyors to His Royal Highness King Victoria". On the labels of authentic Scotch whisky Victoria instead vied for pride of place with Mary Queen of Scots, national heroine and 'martyr'.

From 1644 onwards the history of Scotch whisky was conditioned by taxes imposed by the English on home-distilled spirits. The ensuing contention between excisemen of the Crown and Scots, who operated illegal stills, further aggravated the long-standing antagonism between the two countries. What started as a battle over taxes turned eventually - and inevitably - into a political battle, summed up in the words of the great Robert Burns: "Freedom and Whisky gang thegither". The illegal whisky distilleries - source of celebrated labels like Glen Grant and The Glenlivet - eventually became a solid part of

Scottish tradition. Initially the law allowed only aristocracy to produce distillates but, with barley, peat and water so plentiful, pot-stills were installed far and wide. By the end of the 17th century there was already a large number of (mostly illegal) distilleries in operation: of the 408 existing in Edinburgh in 1777, only eight were officially sanctioned. The wily Highlanders soon learnt to deal with unannounced visits from the excisemen: as soon as they had word of their presence in the area, the 'black pot' (the illegal pot-still recalled in the popular toast "blessed be the black pot and cursed the men who go looking for it") was taken apart and concealed. Getting rid of the malted barley left after fermentation was not so simple. Had it been thrown in the river, the excisemen could have followed the trail upstream and found the still. The problem was solved, after dark, by the sheep of an unknowing farmer, led by their shepherds to demolish this savoury feast. The herdsmen who transported the whisky, well hidden in the midst of their flock, and the women who carried it in small tin containers tucked underneath the folds of their full skirts were instead well in the know. This game of hide-and-seek served only to encourage the Scots to make even better use of their fertile imagination. In the 18th century, for instance, astute Highlanders received cash payments for turning in their old, illicit stills to the excisemen, and promptly used the money to buy new ones. Scotland's largest landowner, the fifth Duke of Gordon (who also ended up on a whisky label...) proposed that whisky production be legalized: the Excise Act of 1823 reduced taxes and led to the opening of a large number of legal distilleries.

Whisky was first used by Celtic monks for therapeutic purposes and its reputation as the miracle-working 'water of life' has remained intact through the centuries. In 1505, the Guild of Surgeons in Edinburgh was granted a monopoly on its distillation. In the 1930's the British Medical Association maintained that four glasses of whisky a day kept heart problems at bay. And people have long considered it the infallible, self-prescribed remedy for colds: "Pour a glass of whisky, put a hat at the foot of your bed and drink until you see two of them".

Scotch whisky, one of Britain's leading exports, is second to none. It is made using a perfect and unique combination of water, peat and micro-climate. But its secret lies in the

22 *Not until the 19th century, when Queen Victoria was consumed by an overwhelming passion for this neglected outpost of her empire, did Scottish people at large adopt kilts, tartan, tam o'shanters, eagle-feathers, sporrans and the like as national symbols. Until then this traditional garb had been worn exclusively by the long ill-suffered Highlanders, from the mountainous Highland region.*

23 *The famous Highland Games were originally a means of enabling clan chieftains to select strong bodyguards. Now, from May to September, more than a hundred of these traditional gatherings are held throughout Scotland, involving many different contests: feats of strength like tossing the caber and tug o' war, races, playing of bagpipes, displays of Scottish dancing, with all the contestants wearing typical Highland dress. The biggest and best known event is the Braemar Games which, since Queen Victoria's day, has always been attended by members of the Royal Family.*

production process itself: to make malt whisky, barley (not necessarily produced locally) is left to germinate, dried over a peat fire, milled and mixed with warm water. With the addition of yeast, the sugars in the 'wort' thus produced are turned into alcohol during fermentation. Lastly the fermented wort is boiled in traditional copper pot-stills, a process carried out twice, usually in two linked stills (in Ireland a triple-distillation system is used). Then come years of maturation in oak casks, preferably previously used to hold Spanish sherry. Every year during ageing the equivalent of about 160 million bottles is lost through evaporation: the so-called "angels' share" (although anyone who has "partaken" of this share may well have seen more nymphs and gnomes than angels).

There are two types of Scotch whisky: malt whisky, made exclusively from malted barley, and grain whisky, made from malted barley, barley and corn. Most brands are blends (generally 60% grain, 40% malt). Blended whiskies, which currently account for 95% of sales, date back to 1853. Their birth is to be attributed to a certain Andrew Usher: he blended a pungent Highland malt with grain spirit produced in a continuous-distillation still patented by Aeneas Coffey and the whisky thus produced gave the Scots a lead over their Irish competitors. Created for delicate English palates, blended whiskies made their mark worldwide, assisted by advertising on a huge scale by prominent Scottish whisky barons like John Dewar, John Buchanan of Black & White, James Mackay of White Horse, Johnnie Walker and John Haig. As their empire grew, so whisky became increasingly well-established as a high-class drink. For the whisky industry these halcyon days came to an abrupt end with World War I when the barley crop was needed strictly for food. There was a further serious setback in 1920 with the introduction of Prohibition in the USA where, thanks also to the many immigrants, whisky was a very popular drink. The Scots were not easily daunted: descendants of well-practised whisky-smugglers, they opened up branches in Cuba, the Bahamas, Bermuda and Canada and, while Ireland was caught up with problems at home, grabbed the lion's share of the illicit liquor market. One devil-may-care bottler even torpedoed his whisky straight onto the beaches of Long Island; picked up by local 'partners in crime' (washerwomen who hid the bottles in their baskets), and the bootleg whisky eventually found its way onto the counters of illegal drinking joints. By 1933, when prohibition was abolished, Scotch whisky was established as a firm favourite and today it is still the most popular whisky in the world. A bottle of whisky from one of Scotland's hundred or so distilleries is opened in the USA every tenth of a second. The Highland distilleries produce a full-bodied whisky, with spicy malts prevailing in the north and fruity ones in the south. Other producing regions are the Lowlands, Islay (malts noted for their well-peated, iodine-like character) and Campbeltown. The best known distilleries are located close to the rivers Spey and Livet, while most of the blends are produced in the area between Glasgow and Edinburgh. Drambuie - the celebrated sweet whisky liqueur (its ingredients can reportedly be traced back to Bonnie Prince Charlie himself) - comes from the Isle of Skye. An ideal pilgrimage for connoisseurs of the "hard stuff" is offered by Scotland's Whisky Trail: an outstanding tour of distilleries which takes in The Glenlivet, Glenfiddich, Macallan and many other famous labels.

Scotland is an amalgam of many landscapes and seascapes: the mountains and moors of the Highlands (home of the camera-shy Loch Ness monster, known affectionately as Nessie), the central Lowlands, the fishing villages of Fife, the vast archipelagos of the Hebrides, the far-northerly Orkney and Shetland Islands, the granite city of Aberdeen overlooking the North Sea, capital of Britain's oil industry. Scotland is much more than the stereotypical image it presents to tourists, comprised of golf courses, Highland Games (traditional day-long pseudo-athletic contests), distilleries and mostly still unspoilt nature. As well as the romantic inland lochs and glens of the Grampians or the heathered hills and empty beaches of Dumfries and Galloway, the country has many cultural attractions. Close to England, the Borders are a beautiful region, its praises often sung by Sir Walter Scott; its prosperity hinged on the wool industry and fabrics such as tweeds and tartans. Here traces can be seen of St. Columba, traditionally credited with converting Scotland to Christianity, as well as of the Picts, driven out by the Scots in 843. Botanical gardens have been planted along the rugged western coast of Argyll, which is warmed by the Gulf Stream and there are

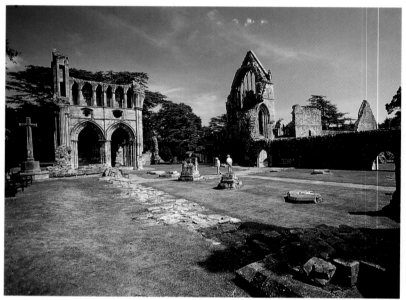

24 top *Stirling, main town of the Central region, is looked upon as the "gateway to the Highlands". Its imposing castle, built on a volcanic crag, was long considered one of Scotland's most impregnable fortresses. Another noteworthy building is the late Gothic Church of the Holy Rude, its crenellated tower and secluded graveyard commanding a splendid view over the town. Here, at the tender age of one, James VI, son of Mary Queen of Scots, was crowned King of Scotland.*

24 bottom *Dryburgh Abbey stands in a tranquil spot on the banks of the River Tweed. At the time when it was founded by King David I in 1140, it was one of the Borders' four main abbeys. It survived numerous raids but was almost totally destroyed in 1544, by order of Henry VIII. Buried here is Sir Walter Scott (1832), Sheriff in the nearby town of Selkirk and author of the many historical novels which, in the 19th century, helped create the myth of the Scottish Highlands.*

25 *The abbey of Culross, with its elegant central tower, was founded in 1217 by Malcolm, earl of Fife, in a position overlooking the town, to house a community of Cistercian monks. Once well-known for the hand-crafted belts made here, Culross is among Scotland's most fascinating towns: thanks to restoration work financed by the Scottish National Trust, it still preserves the character of a 17th/18th-century burgh.*

Norman castles and abbeys, buildings designed along neo-classical lines by William and Robert Adams and in Art Nouveau style by Charles Rennie Mackintosh. There are also 'relics' of the industrial revolution (to which a major contribution, invention of the steam engine, was made by another Scot, James Watt).

When at its height in the 18th/19th centuries, industrialization changed the face of Glasgow, making it - population-wise - the second-largest city of the British Empire. Since the last century, when it was the business capital of Scotland, Glasgow has undergone a further facelift: previously renowned for its shipbuilding and steel industries, it is now better known for its parks, museums and art galleries. Gothic Revival and Victorian architecture mingles happily with the warehouses of old tobacco factories and cotton mills, now converted into fashionable stores and eating places. The focal point of its exhilarating cultural scene (Glasgow was European Capital of Culture, 1990) is the Burrell Collection, one of the most prestigious art collections in the world. Cosmopolitan and no less lively is the handsome city of Edinburgh. Its celebrated annual Arts Festival has played a determining part in drawing the world's attention to its role as capital. The institutions of state held here are law (no appeal can be made against sentences passed by the High Court of Justice) and the church (the independent Church of Scotland is based here). Like 'Doctor Jekyll and Mr Hyde' (written here by Robert Louis Stevenson, a native of the city), Edinburgh is a capital with two souls. High up, dominated by the massive bulk of the Castle, is the dark, medieval Old Town; at the foot of the hill stands the neo-classical New Town, the largest district of Georgian housing in the whole of Britain. Scotland has produced many great men, amongst them David Hume, philosopher; Adam Smith, economist; Alexander Fleming, bacteriologist and discoverer of penicillin; David Livingstone, explorer; James Maxwell, physicist; Graham Bell, inventor of the telephone. It has also kindled the fantasy world of the young (even today's streetwise kids) with captivating stories like Stevenson's *Treasure Island*, Scott's *Ivanhoe* and - especially - J.M.Barrie's *Peter Pan*. All this explains why the reputedly dour Scotland knows how to set us dreaming, and still nurtures dreams of its own.

26-27 A short way from the north-west coast, near the village of Poolewe, Loch Maree is considered among the most beautiful of Scotland's countless freshwater lochs.

28-29 Home of the chiefs of the Macleod Clan for more than 700 years, Dunvegan Castle is built on a rocky outcrop overlooking the loch of the same name, on the island of Skye.

Across heather-clad moors

30 *Two delightful pictures of the farmlands of Fife, one of the twelve regions into which Scotland was divided when its local government structure changed in 1975 (it was previously organized in thirty-three counties, with councils at county, city and burgh levels). The largest region is now Strathclyde, which includes the districts of Argyll, Ayr, Bute, Dumbarton, Lanark and Renfrew.*

31 *Dramatically perched on a rocky headland high above the sea, the ruins of Dunnottar castle - ancient residence of the marshalls of Scotland - are a spectacular sight. Many covenantors (adherents of the Scottish National Covenant of 1638) were imprisoned in this place and, later in the 17th century, the Honours of Scotland, the regalia of the Scottish royal household, were hidden here to save them from Cromwell's troups.*

Ben Nevis, snowy roof of Scotland

32-33 *In the cold light of winter Ben Nevis (at 4,400 feet, Britain's highest mountain) on the east side of the Great Glen, has a distinctly hostile air. Its peak can nonetheless be reached without great difficulty (except for the impervious north face) along a series of well-beaten tracks. The panorama from the summit* *is stunning, with views sweeping from the Hebrides to the mountains of Torridon, the Cairngorms and Glen Coe. But even in summertime excursions to Ben Nevis are not without risk: the weather in Scotland sometimes changes swiftly and the temperature at the summit can quickly drop below zero.*

Enchanted bays, wild lowlands

34-35 *At the head of Loch Shiel stands the Glenfinnan Monument. This slender column surmounted by the statue of a highlander was erected in 1815 as a memorial to the men who lost their lives fighting for the cause of the ill-fated Bonnie Prince Charlie. It was here, in 1745, that the prince raised the Stuart standard and, with the support of five thousand men of the MacDonald Clan, began his hapless struggle to succeed to the Scottish throne.*

35 *Water - be it in the sea, lochs, rivers or streams - is an omnipresent and vital part of the Scottish landscape. And water is also an essential element of 'uisge beatha', the acquavitae or 'water of life' first distilled in Scotland by Celtic monks and known worldwide as whisky. Scots drink whisky with haggis (the most Scottish of dishes) and at many important moments throughout their lives. Tradition demands that a teaspoonful welcome babies into the world, and several rounds see the deceased on their way into the next. And at Hogmanay (as the Scots call New Year's Eve) whisky symbolizing life - together with salt for prosperity and coal for warmth - accompanies the dark-haired man who, to bring good luck, must be first to cross the threshold of every home. Scotch whisky quickly acquired an image of prestige; it even made an appearance in operas like Puccini's* The Girl of the Golden West *and* Madame Butterfly. *Now the most popular spirit in the world, it represents one of Scotland's most important sources of revenue.*

36-37 In the northernmost part of the Highland region, close to Durness and the fishing village of Tongue, the freezing-cold wind that sweeps across beaches and clifftops - often reaching gale force - is a reminder that the North Pole is not so very far away. This is the realm of puffins, seals, coots, plovers and many sea birds. Not far from Durness are several of the area's main attractions: Smoo Caves (the first of the three caverns can be entered on foot and explored for just over 330 feet), into which tumbles the Alto Smoo stream, creating an underground waterfall; the beautiful beach of Balnakeil, where there is a thriving community of craftsmen skilled in marquetry, woodturning and production of silverwares; a ruined 8th-century church built by St. Maelrubha (who brought the Christian faith to this part of the world) and a small graveyard with some intriguing tombstones.

38-39 Grazing land fronts the deserted, sandy beach of Melvich. The unspoilt nature of Scotland provides a haven for many species of animals which - like the Rum mouse or Soay wild sheep - have gradually developed different characteristics from similar species found in continental Europe. For a number of creatures - wild cat, red grouse, pheasant, red deer and roe deer - the upland terrain of the Highlands and the Grampians provides an ideal habitat.

40-41 *Since 1877 the waterfall on Loch Maree has been named after Queen Victoria: this was when she first visited the loch - a tongue of water 13 miles in length, presided over by mountains more than 3,280 feet high - and was stunned by its beauty. Victoria first "discovered" Scotland, and the Highlands in particular, several decades earlier: in 1848 Sir James Clark, her personal physician, had recommended the dry air of the Scottish mountains as a remedy for the rheumatism which already afflicted the young queen.*

42 *Fish are abundant in the lochs, rivers and burns of Scotland, where salmon and rainbow trout live. Salmon fishing is a prestigious sport practised by seriously wealthy anglers (like the hunters whose quarry is red deer, they come from as far away as the Middle East and North America, as well as Britain and Europe),* willing to spend a small fortune to sate their passion. A week's fishing licence on one of the many 'beats' on rivers like the Spey, Tay, Forss, Tweed and Conon can cost as much as the astronomical sum of 25,000 pounds. Fly-fishing for trout is instead practised in many lochs along the west coast and in the far north.*

42-43 *Highland cattle are renowned for their hardiness and the quality of their meat, now exported to France and Germany. For centuries their feed has included the draff discarded by whisky distilleries. In the 18th century, when illegal Highland distillers were constantly 'at war' with English excisemen, they found a cunning way of eliminating possibly incriminating evidence: the malted barley left after fermentation was fed to livestock (often unknown to the farmer).*

44-45 *There is no better way for tourists to experience the wild natural beauty of Scotland and the hospitality of its people than with "bed & breakfast" in a home or farm deep in the heart of the countryside. Little is now left of the great Caledonian forests of pine and oak that once covered much of this land: great areas were felled by the Vikings and more recently, in the 18th and 19th centuries, huge tracts of forest were cleared to provide pastures on which to rear Cheviot sheep. However, as a result*

of government-promoted reforestation in the early part of this century, incentivated in the Highlands with tax relief for landowners, Scotland now has about 600,000 hectares of forests, about half of them owned by the state.

46-47 *Until 200 years ago Scalloway was the main town of the Shetland Islands; this fishing port (used as a wartime harbour by ships of the Norwegian navy) now has a thriving fish processing industry. Situated in the town is a small museum and the ruins of a 17th-century castle built (but never completed) in medieval style for a grandson of Mary Queen of Scots, the notoriously cruel Earl Patrick Stuart.*

The windswept Orkneys

48 top *About 70 islands (only 23 inhabited) make up the archipelago of the Orkneys; their total population is about 17,000. They are on the same latitude as Greenland but have the Gulf Stream to thank for their mild, temperate climate. In winter the temperature in Kirkwall, main town of Mainland, the largest island, is much the same as in London. Along their coasts are rugged cliffs and protected bays; inland, the treeless, hilly terrain is extensively used for cattle and sheep farming, and for crops: vegetables and cereals.*

48 bottom *Like the Shetlands, the Orkneys were Norse dominions for many centuries. Only in 1472, when they were part of the dowry offered to James III by the Norwegian princess Margaret, did they become part of Scotland. A great many species of seabirds come to nest here, on cliffs in the nine nature reserves protected by the Royal Society for the Protection of Birds: this picture is of the reserve at Marvich Head, with its Kitchener Memorial tower, on Mainland island. Not surprisingly, the Orkneys are much frequented by ornithologists and birdwatchers.*

49 *The first settlements in the Orkneys date back almost 5,000 years. A remarkable testimonial to the history of these isles is the Ring of Brogar, on Mainland island: this great circle of 36 stones (originally there were 60) formed a ring about 985 feet in diameter, surrounded by a ditch. While the function of the stones (believed to be as old as Egypt's pyramids) can be only conjectured, they are undoubtedly a breathtaking sight.*

50-51 *Skye is the best known island of the Inner Hebrides. Together with the Outer Hebrides - also called the Western Isles - the archipelago comprises over 500 mostly uninhabited islands. Situated like the rest of the Hebridean islands in an ancient volcanic region, Skye has a landscape characterized by valleys and* high peaks (particularly renowned are its Cuillin Hills, not far from the south-east coast), mainly of granite rock. As well as tourism, fishing and farming, a major contribution to Skye's economy comes from production of tweed: cloth made from pure Scottish wool, until 1930 still coloured with vegetable dyes.

52-53 *Covering an area of 643 square miles (with a length of almost 50 miles and a width of 32, at the widest point), Skye is the largest of the Hebridean islands. The approximately 8,000 people who make up its population speak mainly Gaelic.*

54-55 *The wind soon chases away clouds hiding the sun over one of the splendid sandy beaches situated on Harris, the southern part of the largest of the Outer Hebrides (Harris and Lewis, to the north, are a single island). Besides sheep farming, the islanders' activity is focused on Harris tweed, still a cottage industry based on weavers working in their own homes.*

Culture and business in the heart of Scotland

56 top *Partly hidden by the bridge over the River Kelvin and thick vegetation are the buildings of Glasgow University, the second oldest in the region, founded by Bishop Turnbull in 1451. Adam Smith, one of the forerunners of economic liberalism, taught here from 1751 to 1763. One of his most illustrious students was James McGill (1744-1813), who, as recalled in a commemorative stone in the cloister of the university, eventually founded the University of Montreal in Canada, named after him.*

56 bottom and 57 *Two of the most characteristic panoramas of Edinburgh: the first shows part of Princes Street at dusk; the second is the cityscape seen from the vantage point of the Camera Obscura. With its many shops and department stores, Princes Street is the main shopping area of Scotland's capital city. About a mile long, it separates the Old Town from the New (built on the north side of the castle between 1760 and 1840).*

Edinburgh, gracious capital city

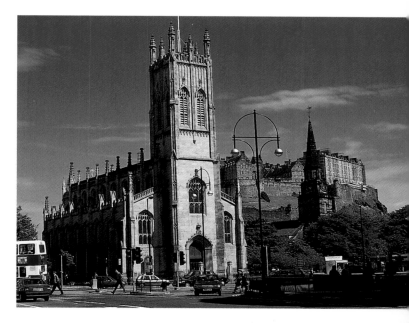

58-59 *Towering over North Bridge is the imposing bulk of the Castle, a collection of buildings erected at different times in history and used through the centuries as the city's fortress, armoury, arsenal and prison. Thanks to Malcolm III Canmore, the monarch who elevated Edinburgh to capital of Scotland, from the 11th century onwards it was also seat of the monarchy.*

59 top right *Partly concealed in this view by St. John's Church is Edinburgh Castle, one-time stronghold of the Picts, rebuilt in the 6th century by Edwin, king of Northumberland. A strategic site many times contended by Scots and English, it stands 377 feet above sea level, on the top of a steep and rugged volcanic hill.*

59 left and 59 bottom right *Another view of Edinburgh's Old Town, stretches from the Castle Rock to the royal palace of Holyroodhouse. The finest panoramic view of the city can be had from the observation platform of the Camera Obscura, built in 1850 in the Outlook Tower.*

60-61 *St. Giles' Cathedral was built between 1387 and 1450 in Gothic style (it was modelled on the Cathedral Church of St. Nicolas in Newcastle upon Tyne) on the site of a previous Romanesque church. Since then it has been restructured several times. For only two brief periods in the 17th century, under Charles I and Charles II, was the ancient church actually an Episcopal cathedral but it has retained the name. Among its features are the tomb of the Marquess of Montrose (pictured here) and the Chapel of the Thistle (the photo highlights a detail of its vault); only the Knights of the Thistle, an exclusive Scottish order with 16 members plus the reigning monarch, have the privilege of worshipping here. Over the archway into the chapel are two characteristic Scottish motifs: thistle and bagpipes (with an angel piper).*

David

The Lord is my light and my salvation

62-63 *These close-ups reveal the splendour of the stained-glass windows that are a major decorative feature of the High Kirk of St. Giles (kirk is the Gaelic word for church), also - incorrectly - called St. Giles' Cathedral. Several are works of two highly talented and very well-known designer/craftsmen, William Morris and Edward Burne-Jones.*

64-65 *The Palace of Holyroodhouse, in the foreground, and a panoramic view of the city. Erected on the site of a 12th-century abbey, the palace was extensively restructured by Sir William Bruce in the late 17th century on commission from Charles II (although the king never actually set foot in the place). It was here that, in 1558, David Rizzio, the Italian secretary (and possibly lover) of Mary Queen of Scots was murdered before the queen's eyes and, in 1745, Bonnie Prince Charlie set up his court. Used by George IV during his 1822 visit to Scotland and later also by Queen Victoria and Prince Albert, it is still the official Edinburgh home of the royal family.*

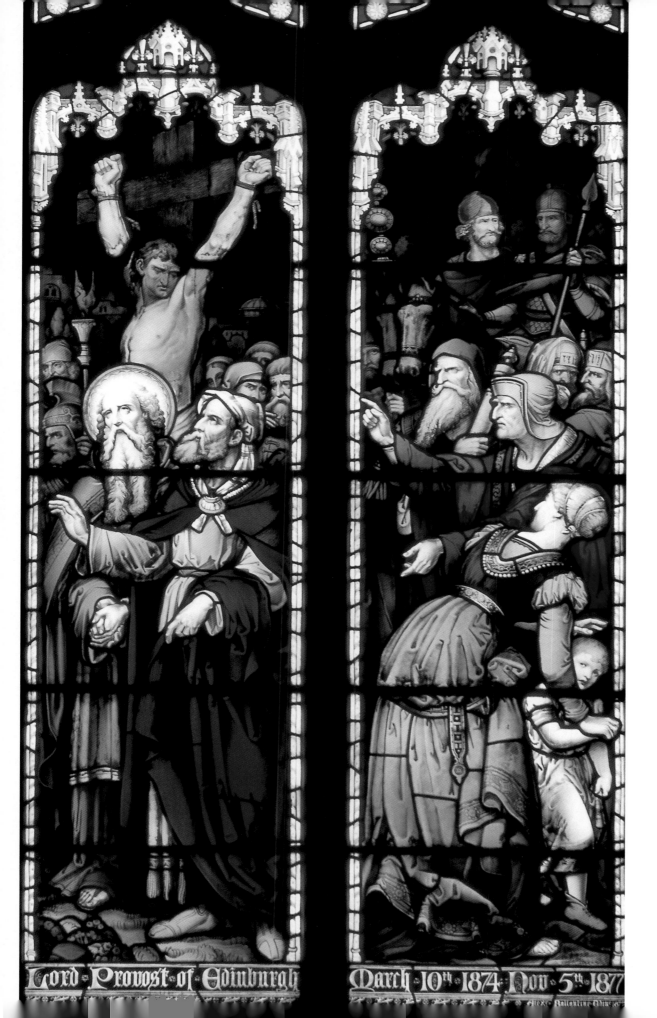

Lord · Provost · of · Edinburgh   March · 10th · 1874 · Nov · 5th · 1877

63

66 and 67 bottom *Three photos taken after dark convey the typical atmosphere of Ryrie & Co., one of the many Edinburgh pubs where people gather to drink beer and socialize. In Scotland, as elsewhere in Britain, pubs also offer meals, often including some local speciality on their bill of fare. Their clientele is a cross-section of the local population, ranging from punks to elderly gentlemen in tweed suits. Opening times are generally 11 a.m. to 11 p.m. (with drinking time extended by an hour to midnight on Fridays and Saturdays). Beer and spirits may be served only to over-18s; under-14s can go into pubs to eat provided they are accompanied by an adult. Rose Street in Edinburgh is well-known for its many pubs.*

67 top *A great place for passing the time of day with friends over a pint or two of beer or a glass of whisky, Bennets Bar in Edinburgh is one of the boasts of Scotland. Savouring whisky here or in other pubs is surely the most authentic way to enjoy this most celebrated of spirits (not produced on a truly industrial scale until 1820). Scots like to drink their whisky in several different ways: neat, with a glass of water or diluted with soda.*

68-69 *The National Gallery of Scotland, in Edinburgh, is housed in a neo-classical building (1822-45) designed, like the nearby Royal Scottish Academy, by the architect William Playfair. Considered one of the finest art collections in the British Isles, the gallery has an outstanding selection of works by great Italian Renaissance, Flemish and Impressionist painters; major Scottish and English painters are, of course, also*

well represented. There are paintings by Raphael, Titian, Rubens, Perugino, Goya, Rembrandt, van Dyck, but also Cézanne, Turner, Monet and Degas. Scottish artists represented include Raeburn, Ramsay, Paton and Drummond.

Glasgow, engine of Scotland

70 *Glasgow boasts not one but two universities: the old and illustrious Glasgow University, in the Kelvingrove Park area, and Strathclyde University, a former Polytechnic.*

71 *West George Road is one of the busiest thoroughfares in Glasgow. Towards the end of the 1700's the city grew at a tremendous pace, also to accommodate tens of thousands of immigrants who came to work in the cotton mills which replaced the previously flourishing tobacco industry.*

72-73 Within the confines of the university a long-established custom continues: in keeping with tradition, many Scottish marriages are celebrated beneath the neo-Gothic vaults of the university chapel. The bride, as can be seen, is conventionally attired; the groom and male guests wear ceremonial dress, with kilts in their clan tartan. Glasgow University has seen many great names within its hallowed walls - the economist Adam Smith, for instance, was a teacher here - and the city is still a symbol of the inventive talents of the Scottish people. In the 18th and 19th centuries an extraordinary number of outstanding men lived and worked here: Adam Ferguson (a forerunner of modern sociology), John Napier (inventor of logarithms), James Hutton, Roderick Murchison and Charles Lyell (founders of modern geology), James Clerk Maxwell (who discovered the laws of electrodynamics), Lord Kelvin (main contributor to development of the second law of thermodynamics, whose name is still used as a unit for measuring absolute temperature), William Cullen, John and William Hunter (who revolutionized gynaecology and surgery), Andrew Duncan, James Young (who introduced the use of chloroform in operating theatres) and - best known of all - Alexander Fleming (discoverer of penicillin).

74-75 *The imposing and sedate exterior of Kelvingrove Art Gallery and Museum is softened by its setting: a spacious park to which Glaswegians flock on sunny days. Glasgow was the birthplace of a very prominent architect of the early 1900s: Charles Rennie Mackintosh. An exponent of Art Nouveau, he left many fine works in the city: handsome houses in Sauchiehall Street, the Glasgow School of Art and Queen's Cross Church. Together with drawings and projects, a reconstruction of the Glasgow house that Mackintosh once lived in and furnished, is among the exhibits in the Hunterian Art Gallery, which houses Glasgow University's art collection; his early 20th-century interiors for the Willow Tearooms can instead be seen in Kelvingrove Art Gallery.*

76 centre left *George Square is considered the heart of modern Glasgow. Statues abound here (with figures of Queen Victoria, Prince Albert, James Watt and the national poet, Robert Burns) but pride of place - high up on the central column - has been given to Sir Walter Scott. Fronting the square is City Chambers, the city hall built in Venetian Renaissance style to a design by architect William Young; the building was opened by Queen Victoria in 1888.*

76 bottom left *From Kingston Bridge the monumental face of Glasgow is portrayed in its nocturnal splendour. Back in the Sixties large areas of tenement housing were demolished in an attempt to eliminate suburban slums (infamous for their high infant mortality rate and squalid living conditions) and redevelop other run-down parts of the city. But in many cases urban renewal has brought irreparable changes to the city's original fabric.*

76 top and bottom right *Two of Glasgow's many characteristic eating and drinking places: the Gandolfi café-restaurant in Merchant City, in premises formerly occupied by the old cheese market (self-styled 'café of yesteryear' with elegant and original interior décor), and the Horse Shoe pub. Culturally Glasgow is a very lively city, certainly meriting its nomination as European City of Culture 1990. Events organized here annually include the Mayfest drama festival, an international jazz festival, and a major folk and choral music event. The city is home of the Scottish Opera (at the Theatre Royal), Scottish National Orchestra, Scottish Ballet and the Royal Scottish Academy of Music and Drama. A particularly popular venue is the original Tramway Theatre, housed in an old tram shed, where Peter Brook, among others, has mounted successful productions.*

77 *At dusk Glasgow Cathedral takes on the evocative appearance of an illuminated ship. It was erected between 1123 and 1136 over the tomb of Saint Mungo, patron saint of the city, on the site of a chapel destroyed by fire. Later additions to the building include the Lady's Chapel and the sacresty, completed in the 15th century, and the splendid grille in front of the raised choir, only slightly more recent. Behind the cathedral is the 19th-century Western Necropolis, where many of the city's notables are buried.*

78 *Glaswegians often call in at the Café Rouge and relax briefly in the opulent glass conservatory of the Winter Gardens (now a tearoom) adjoining the People's Palace. This 19th-century redstone building, with allegorical figures decorating its facade, stands in Glasgow Green park. The museum it houses tells the history of Glasgow, Scotland's most important centre of trade and industry (and home to about a fifth of its population).*

79 top *Always a great place to go shopping, Glasgow has recently acquired two huge new shopping centres. Both offer an almost infinite variety of sales outlets, boutiques, eating places and department stores.*

79 bottom *Now standing on the site once occupied by St. Enoch railway station (demolished together with the adjoining hotel), in the square of the same name, is St. Enoch Centre, a futuristic shopping centre created from steel, glass and mirrors.*

80-81 *There is much more to Scotland than the natural beauty of its deservedly renowned scenery. It is also rich in museums and art galleries. As well as the celebrated Burrell Collection (Britain's most important private art collection, donated to the city in 1944 by shipping magnate Sir William Burrell), Glasgow has another exceptional cultural asset: Kelvingrove Art Gallery and Museum (pictured in this photo is the main room), with works by Giorgione* (The Adulteress Brought before Christ), *Botticelli, Rembrandt, Monet, Dali, paintings of French and Dutch schools, as well as collections of silverware, porcelain, arms, sculptures and furniture.*

The black gold of Aberdeen

82 *The Mercat Cross is the old heart of the commercial centre of Aberdeen. Financed by the city corporations, the monument was erected in the square down Union Street back in 1686. Surmounted by a unicorn, the column stands on a hexagonal base bearing coats-of-arms and busts of Stuart monarchs.*

83 Union Street, seen here at sunset, is Aberdeen's main thoroughfare. Situated on the North Sea coast at the mouth of the rivers Don and Dee, this port is Scotland's third largest town in terms of population. The North Sea oil boom of the 1970s brought new importance and prosperity to the city. Now, as well as its traditional industries - fishing, fish processing, livestock and granite exporting (Aberdeen is popularly known as Granite or Silver City, on account of its prevalently silver-grey granite buildings), Aberdeen hosts big offices of leading oil companies.

Inverness,
in the heart of the Highlands

84-85 *In the clear night air Inverness has the typical charm of Northern European cities. Capital of the Highlands, on the Caledonian canal, its strategic position has made the town an important road and rail hub. Its 19th-century castle stands on the site of a medieval fortress. Through the centuries the town has been razed to the ground several times. Among the few tangible remnants of its past is the curious Ciach-na-Cudainn, a stone on which the womenfolk used to set tubs of water filled from the river: according to legend, Inverness will prosper for as long as the stone remains in the town.*

Castles, villages, ghosts

86 top *Viewed here from the harbour at sunset, Oban is a popular summer holiday resort on the west coast (many ferries and cruise ships to the Hebrides set sail from its port). Presiding over the town from a hilltop is the curious McCaig's Folly, an unfinished imitation of Rome's Colosseum: it was started in 1897 by a rich banker (who died before its completion) in an attempt to provide an answer to the problem of local unemployment.*

86 bottom *A famous landmark in Craigellachie, situated at the confluence of the rivers Spey and Fiddich, is the elegant iron bridge built there by Thomas Telford. But the town is best known for its distilleries: malt whisky from the Craigellachie distillery (founded in 1891, it moved to new premises in the 1960s) is used in the White Horse blend. The Macallan distillery, established in 1824, is also located here.*

87 *Crail is a picturesque village of white cottages with red pantiled roofs in Fife, the county of central Scotland washed on three sides by the waters of the North Sea. It was along this coast, famous for its beautiful scenery and its small fishing communities, that Scotland's ancient seafaring traditions first developed.*

The magical charm of centuries-old seaports

88 *Not far from Crail is St. Monance, an ancient burgh where all Fife's fishing boats were once built (but now only yachts). Still standing here, as well as several 18th-century buildings, is St. Monan's Church, erected in about 1362 by order of King David I.*

88-89 *The village pictured in this photo is Macduff, on the southern shore of the Moray Firth, in the county of Banff. Situated in Banff Bay, which is formed*

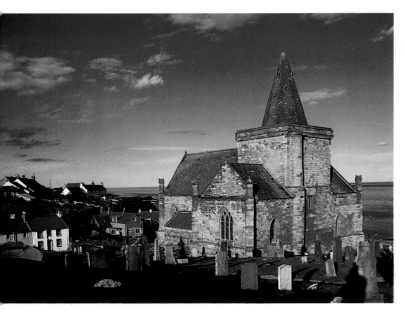

by the delta of the River Deveron, its streets and houses climb up a hillside east of the bay, opposite the town of Banff. Macduff, known until 1783 as Doune, is a busy fishing port, heavily dependent on herrings. Its fishmarket, set up in 1966, should not be missed!

90-91 *Portree is the 'capital' of the Isle of Skye; built on a rocky headland, its colourful cottages overlook a harbour effectively protected by the nearby island of Raasay. The town's original name - Kiltaraglen - was changed in 1540 to Port an Righ, or 'king's port', in honour of James V. In Portree, as elsewhere on the island, Sunday is respected as a day of rest.*

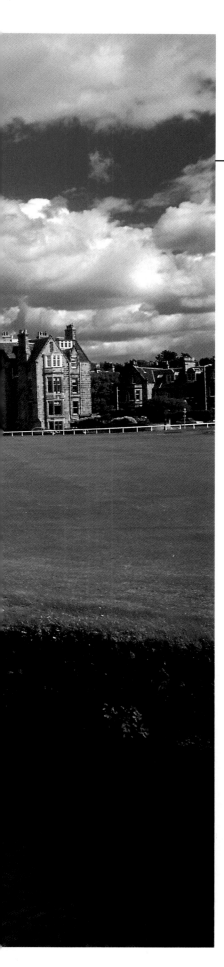

St.Andrews, golfing mecca

92-93 and 93 top *The impeccable greens of the world's most celebrated golf course, at the Royal and Ancient Golf Club of St. Andrews, draw champions and novices alike. The prestige of this golfing mecca - founded on May 14, 1754 by 22 "Gentlemen of Honour skillful in the ancient and healthfull exercise of golf" - is beyond dispute. In 1894 the Club established the international rules of golf which are still updated and amended here, in agreement with the United States Golf Association. It was at St. Andrews that the prototype of what subsequently became the conventional 18-hole course was first laid out: a 9-hole course played in reverse on the return journey. Practised in Scotland since 1457, golf steadily gained in popularity; during the reign of James II it was banned as a distraction from the noble sport of archery.*

93 centre and bottom *The ruined cathedral and castle are outstanding features of St. Andrews. Built between 1160 and 1318, when the city was the ecclesiastical capital of Scotland, the cathedral is the largest church in the country. It survives only as towering ruins: still standing are the east wall of the choir with an ornate late-Gothic window, parts of the transept, the south wall of the nave, the west façade and the chapter-house, as well as the cemetery. Many supporters of the Reformation were tried here as heretics; the riots instigated by their execution led to the storming of the castle by followers of John Knox and the murder of Cardinal Beaton. Later attacked by the French troops of Mary Queen of Scots, the Protestant rebels were eventually forced to capitulate.*

The ports of Fife

94-95 *In Pittenweem and Anstruther, day-to-day activity centres on the harbour. Pittenweem is the busiest fishing port on the northern side of the Firth of Forth; the many old buildings restored by the National Trust of Scotland add a historic note to the town. The ruins of a 14th-century Augustinian priory are to be found here. Also in neighbouring Anstruther, with its 'vernacular' stone houses, the harbour is the focal point of town life; before 1940, in fact, when herring was still caught in these waters, it was one of the foremost fishing ports of the region. The Scottish Fisheries Museum is now located here, with objects, old photos and paintings telling the story of local fishing and fisherfolk. Another attraction, moored in the harbour, is the North Carr Lightship, stationed off Fife Ness until 1976.*

96-97 *Situated on the northern shore of Loch Broom, the old fishing village of Ullapool was founded in 1788 by the British Fisheries Society as a centre for the herring trade. In recent years, thanks to its mild climate (attributable to the* *warming effects of the Gulf Stream), the nearby lochs and mountains and its harbour (which is a terminal for ferries to the Outer Hebrides and pleasure cruises to the Summer Islands), it has become a popular holiday resort.*

English influence in the Borders

98-99 *The abbey church of the Holy Trinity is the cathedral of the city of Dunfermline, built on the north side of the River Forth and known for its textile production (silk and damask). Founded in 1070 by Margaret of England, wife of Malcolm III Canmore, the abbey was destroyed by the English*

in 1303. Burial place of Robert the Bruce - one of the nation's great warrior heroes, king of Scotland from 1307 to 1329 - the church has a Romanesque nave with handsome columns and arched doorways and windows. The neo-Gothic choir and lantern were added after 1820.

99 top and bottom *As well as golf and rugby, cricket and bowls are very popular sports in Scotland. The names of many Scots are inscribed in the annals of sporting history and the country's mountains, lochs and coastal waters offer plenty of opportunities to practise sport: skiing (the main ski resorts are in*

Aviemore, Glencoe, Glenshee and The Lecht, but Britain's longest artificial piste is at Hillend, in the Pentland Hills), trekking, climbing (over 280 mountains rise above 2950 feet), diving (around Oban, Ullapool and St.Abbs Head) and even surfing (at Thurso and between Bettyhill and John O'Groats, on the north coast).

Whisky and bagpipes

100-101 *Certain stereotyped facets of Scotland that have brought it fame worldwide: for instance, the drone of bagpipes and the symbolic movements typical of Scottish dances (such as the celebrated Highland Fling, in which raised arms recall the horns of the red deer). They acquired legendary status after the traditional dress and customs of* the Highlands were brought into vogue by Queen Victoria in the 19th century. Since then Scots generally have been happy to adopt them as their own. Besides bagpipes, the violin and Scottish harp are traditional Scottish musical instruments, often played at folk festivals which - after catching on in the Sixties - now take place on many weekends between Easter and Autumn.

102 *Considered one of Scotland's oldest, Strathisla distillery at Keith, in the Highland region, was founded in 1786 although a farm where whisky was distilled reportedly existed here many years before. One of the most prominent features of this handsome granite building is the distinctive pagoda roofs of the kilns used to dry the malted barley, typical of malt whisky distilleries; it also has a small room containing the traditional pot-stills. The malt whisky produced here is not easy to find, most of it being used for the splendid Chivas Regal de Luxe blends.*

103 top left *Time-honoured traditions hold good in the casks warehouse of the Glenfiddich distillery in Dufftown, Speyside. Owned by the Grant-Gordon family, descendants of William Grant, it is the only distillery equipped to bottle its own single malts. A small museum and a beautifully organized still house complete a tour during which visitors see every stage of the distilling process.*

103 bottom left and 103 right *Pictured here at the Dalwhinnie distillery - in the village of the same name, on Speyside in the Highlands - are huge fermentation vats made from Douglas fir or larch, and enormous pot-stills (their shape and size make a determining contribution to the flavour of the whisky). This distillery is the highest in Scotland: originally called Stratspey Distillery, it was built here in 1897 close to an old stopping place frequented by cattle traders. Destroyed by fire, it was rebuilt in 1934. The subtly-peated malt whisky produced here has a light, aromatic fragrance and is used in the Buchanan blends, Black & White for instance.*

Bastions of the north

104-105 *The last rays of the setting sun illuminate the pleasant town of Stirling, administrative centre of the Central region, situated on the banks of the River Forth. Presiding over the town from a rocky outcrop is the age-old grey stone castle, for many centuries a favourite residence of Stuart monarchs who sought refuge here on numerous occasions (its walls witnessed the deaths of kings Alexander I (1124) and William I the Lion (1214), and the birth of James III and possibly also of James IV, while James V spend his childhood years here).*

Mystery and magic of the Highlands

106-107 *The three castles pictured here are all famous but differ in their history and architecture. Two are representative examples of Scottish baronial style, an offshoot of the British Gothic Revival introduced in the 19th century to counter foreign influence: Thirlestane (top) with its elegant turrets, and the magical Eilean Donan (right), its majestic forms seemingly emerging from the waters of the surrounding Loch Long. The country houses of Scotland have often developed from simple medieval fortified towers, built on manmade hills encircled by palisades and ditches; whether sturdy or elegant, low-lying or sky-high, they now form an integral part of the most evocative Scottish landscapes. Situated in the county of Berwick, Mellerstain House (bottom) is instead a typical Georgian residence; the work of the celebrated Adams, it was started in 1725 by William Adam and completed in 1788 by his son, Robert. It is a lovely house of sedate, classical design, its interiors featuring stuccowork, pastel colours and neo-classical ornamentation; it also has a terraced Italianate garden.*

Sentinels of history

108-109 *Shown here are examples of how the works of nature and man can complement and enhance one another, creating scenes of rare beauty. Much of the dramatic appeal of the 15th-century Dunnottar Castle stems from the rocky headland it stands on which makes it seem even more wild and desolate. Somewhat less picturesque are the ruins of Slains castle,*

close to Aberdeen, or the austere-looking Caerlaverock Castle, south of Dumfries. Triangular in shape, Caerlaverock was built in 1290 for its first owner, Earl Maxwell of Nithsdale. It was renovated in 1460 and again in 1634 but only six years later, after a long seige, parts of it were abandoned and left to fall into ruins. The medieval external appearance of the castle belies its interiors: dated 1650, they are in Renaissance style.

110 Not far from Kelso stands Floors
Castle, in Gothic-Baroque style, still the
property of its original owners, the Dukes of
Roxburghe. Designed by William Adam in
the late 18th century with plentiful spires,
chimney-pots and gargolyes, it was extended
in the Victorian period by W.H. Playfair
who gave full reign to his imagination,
adding further turrets and chimneys.
Several scenes of the film Greystoke were
shot here. As well as furniture from the
17th and 18th centuries and a series of
French tapestries, the castle contains a
valuable collection of modern paintings.

111 Near the village of Fyvie, Fyvie Castle stands in the midst of extensive grounds that include a lake. It has undergone many changes from its original 13th-century structure; in particular it has acquired five towers, each added by one of its various resident families. It underwent its last facelift in the 19th century. Housed in the castle is an outstanding collection of paintings, including portraits by Raeburn and Gainsborough.

A castle fit for Queens

112-113 *The interiors of the fairytale castle of Glamis abound with boiseries, hunting trophies and furniture dating from the 14th to 19th centuries. In the flower-decked dining room where official banquets are held the table is always laid. Displays of fresh flowers also decorate the bedroom of the Queen Mother, Lady Elizabeth Bowes-Lyon. Glamis was her childhood home (as it was for the present Queen Elizabeth) and it was here, in 1930, that she gave birth to her daughter Margaret. A particularly impressive*

sight, in the wing added in the late 18th century, is the billiard room in which a still-life by Rubens takes pride of place. It is apparently in the chapel, embellished with wood panelling and paintings of biblical scenes, that one of the castle's ghosts makes her appearances: tradition has it that the far left-hand corner is haunted by the Lady in Grey, ill-fated protagonist of a tragic love story. She is one of many ghosts - among them Lord Crawford and Jack the Runner - said to have made Glamis their permanent home.

114-115 *Glamis Castle is located near Forfar, main town of the county of Angus. The 14th-century tower house that was its original core has been transformed through the years, with extensive additions made in the 17th and 19th centuries.*

112

Stirling, fortress of dishonour

116-117 *Standing high on Gowan Hill to the north-west of Stirling, 'bastion of the north', are the imposing grey stone walls of Stirling Castle. The town has always been of strategic importance (it is positioned on the imaginary line connecting the northern and southern halves of Scotland) and its castle has been the scene of many battles. For a long time used as barracks, it was occupied by the Erskines, knight commanders of the king. The castle walls enclose several mainly 15th- and 16th-century buildings: a palace, built in 1460-1540 in Renaissance style with an inner courtyard enhanced by large statues (including a Scottish soldier and somewhat grotesque figures of a king, queen and chamberlain), the 15th-century Parliament Hall and the Chapel Royal, added in the 17th century. Other highlights of the castle are the Regimental Museum of the Argyll and Sutherland Highlanders and the notorious 15th-century Douglas Hall: here King James II murdered the 8th Earl of Douglas (to whom he had previously granted a safe-conduct), throwing his body from a window into the garden below.*

117

Blair,
stronghold of the Atholl Highlanders

118-119 *Blair Castle, in the Grampian mountains of Perthshire, owes its present appearance to a series of complete renovations: the stairway with the family portrait gallery, for instance, was added in 1756. After a period of occupation by Jacobite troops under the command of Graham of Claverhouse, in 1689 the castle was left semi-destroyed. Between 1869 and 1904 the whole building was radically restructured. The castle has many splendid features, notably the ballroom, the entrance hall decorated with hunting trophies, shields, swords, bows and guns, and the baroque dining hall.*

120-121 *The origins of Blair Castle date back to the mid-13th century. For practically the last four hundred years the castle has been the seat of the Dukes of Atholl. The duke is the only man in Britain allowed to retain a private army, a right granted by Queen Victoria: once a year the Atholl Highlanders hold a ceremonial parade here.*

Scone Palace and the Stone of Destiny

122-123 *Scone Palace stands in vast grounds on the outskirts of Perth, administrative centre of Perthshire, on the banks of the river Tay. It is built on the site of the abbey of Scone, destroyed in the mid-16th century by followers of Protestant Reformist John Knox; the Stone of Scone - the so-called Stone of Destiny, upon which kings of Scotland were crowned - was kept here until 1297, when Edward I of England defeated the Scots and removed the stone to Westminster Abbey (where it remains to this day). Now home of the 8th Earl of Mansfield, the present turreted mansion was erected in the late 16th century and renovated in 1802. Its many treasures include embroidery work by Mary Queen of Scots and a writing bureau once owned by Queen Marie-Antoinette. Ornate stucco mouldings embellish the dining room and so-called Embassador's room (one of the earls of Mansfield held this office at the court of the French King Louis XVI). Displayed in the library is a fine collection of old German, French and Chinese porcelain wares. In the park surrounding the palace are a chapel and small graveyard.*

Scottish baronial style

124-125 *At the core of Crathes Castle, near Aberdeen, is a 16th-century tower-house to which substantial extensions were later added. Like practically every self-respecting stately home in Scotland, it is reputedly haunted by a ghost.*

125 left *Close to the town of Galashiels, Abbotsford House was built in Scottish baronial style in 1817-21 by Sir Walter Scott, romantic author of historical novels about Scotland's glorious past. It is now a museum devoted to his life and works.*

128 *Watching over Scotland's north-western shores is Neist Point lighthouse, on the Isle of Skye. Misty Island, as it is also known, is about 50 miles long and 32 wide. With its wild, rugged coastline, it is considered one of the most fascinating of the Scottish islands.*

125 top right *The distinctive feature of 17th-century Fraser Castle is its curious Z-shaped plan; a short way from Aberdeen, it stands in ten hectares of grounds.*

125 bottom right *Some 13 miles from Aberdeen, the elegant 13th-century keep of Drum Castle was extended with two new wings - in 1619 and in the Victorian period - thus acquiring its present very evident U-shaped structure.*

126-127 *In Scotland's far north, close to the coastal town of Brora, stands the picturesque Dunrobin Castle - seat of the Dukes of Sutherland - with its large Italianate gardens. Built on a natural terrace above the sea, its original core dates from the 13th century; it was extended in baronial style in 1844 by Sir Charles Barry, the architect best known for the Houses of Parliament and Tower Bridge in London.*

All pictures inside the book are by Massimo Borchi except the following:

Stefano Ardito:
pages 32, 33

Gianna e Tiziana Baldizzone.
pages 54-55.

Anne Conway:
pages 49, 100-101.

Annamaria Molli / Focus Team:
pages 20-21, 23 top.

Photo Bank:
pages 22, 23 bottom.

Andrea Pistolesi:
page 48.

A. Ponzio / Overseas:
page 46-47.